P9-CQG-184

Fight of the Century

Century

ALICE PAUL BATTLES
WOODROW WILSON
FOR THE VOTE

BARB ROSENSTOCK
Illustrations by SARAH GREEN

CALKINS CREEK
AN IMPRINT OF BOYDS MILLS & KANE
New York

Alice Paul vs.

ALICE STOKES PAUL

Born: January 11, 1885

Hometown: Mt. Laurel Township, New Jersey

Family: Oldest of four children born to banker William Paul and Tacie Parry, a descendant of William Penn, the Quaker founder of Pennsylvania. Single.

Training: Moorestown Friends School, Swarthmore College, University of Pennsylvania, Woodbrooke Quaker Study Center (Birmingham, England)

Previous Matches: Alice fought alongside British suffragists Christabel and Emmeline Pankhurst and wound up arrested seven times for protesting in England. This is her first big fight back home in the United States.

Inspiration: "Unless women are prepared to fight politically they must be content to be ignored politically." —Alice Paul

Woodrow Wilson

THOMAS WOODROW WILSON

Born: December 28, 1856

Hometown: Staunton, Virginia

Family: The third of four children born to minister Joseph Ruggles Wilson and Janet "Jessie" Woodrow. Married, three daughters.

Training: Davidson College, Princeton University, University of Virginia, Johns Hopkins University

Previous Matches: Woodrow struggled to learn to read, winning that ability at the age of ten. While president of Princeton University, Professor Wilson fought an easy first match to become governor of New Jersey. He then fought three experienced opponents—President William Taft, socialist Eugene Debs, and former president Theodore Roosevelt—to win election as the twenty-eighth president of the United States.

Inspiration: "The man who is swimming against the stream knows the strength of it."—Woodrow Wilson

THE CHALLENGER

In this corner, standing five feet six inches, one hundred pounds, wearing long skirts and a large-brimmed hat, women's rights leader, Alice Paul!

This fight determines whether the women of the United States

THE CHAMPION

In this corner, standing five feet eleven inches, weighing 170 pounds, wearing a wool suit and oval glasses, the president-elect of the United States, Woodrow Wilson!

can vote, folks. The winner changes the country forever.

ROUND ONE

The fight starts before Woodrow knows it. The day before his inauguration as president, he steps off the train in Washington, DC, expecting cheering crowds to greet him . . . and almost no one is there.

Where are all the people?

. . . at Alice's parade.

On March 3, 1913, twenty-six floats, nine bands, and more than five thousand women from almost every state march up Pennsylvania Avenue. They wave brilliant silk banners—*Votes for Women. We Want the Vote. We Demand an Amendment.*

Alice heads the parade committee. She marches with college women in caps and gowns topped with purple and gold suffrage sashes. She's done it! The largest protest ever seen in the nation's capital.

DEMAND VOTE

VOTES FOR WOMEN

For more than fifty years, many women and some men worked to change each state's suffrage laws so that women might vote. Still, women vote in just a few states. Alice leads a group of women tired of waiting. They want the new president's attention. They want Congress to pass an amendment to the Constitution. They want America's women to get the vote, NOW!

Vote? Woodrow's head spins. *Proper ladies shouldn't even march in public!*

Alice knocks the wind right out of him.

DING! END OF ROUND ONE.

IN WOODROW'S CORNER

A crowd lines the parade route, half a million strong. Angry men spill into the street. They push, pinch, spit, and throw lit cigars at the marchers. *Go home where you belong!* The suffrage parade dissolves into a riot. Hundreds are injured.

Woodrow knows the best place to fight back. At *his* house. The White House.

On March 17, 1913, Alice and four other suffragists march into the vast East Room. Alice arranges her skirts and gets ready to meet the new president Woodrow Wilson head on.

The president enters with a smile. He shakes Miss Paul's hand. *Such small hands! Such a ladylike dress!* He expects a tougher opponent. *This should be quick.*

Woodrow stands.

The women sit.

He lectures.

They listen.

The president never thinks about votes for women. The president works on important issues. The ladies must let him get back to running the country.

Then Alice steps up. She hurls arguments left and right.

What is more important than democracy? What is more important than freedom? The president must support votes for women . . . or else.

The president backs off reeling. But the round isn't over yet.

Alice keeps Woodrow on his toes. She sends more suffragists to meet him. And more.

Almost every month, Woodrow spars with groups of ladies who want to vote.

Some stand while *he* sits.

Others lecture while *he* listens.

And he hates it.

So he ducks. He dodges. For three years, Woodrow
fights back in the simplest way possible: he ignores them.

DING! END OF ROUND TWO.

IN ALICE'S CORNER

Suffragists hammer Congress with a "Votes for Women" petition over eighteen thousand feet long. They swing a huge banner off the balcony during Woodrow's annual address to Congress.

They shift their headquarters right across from the White House—Woodrow can see the suffrage flag from his daughters' bedrooms. And still, there are no votes for women.

Alice strikes back in a brand new way: with silence. On January 10, 1917, Alice and eleven others march to the White House gates. They hold poles hung with heavy banners—*Mr. President, What Will You Do for Woman Suffrage? How Long Must Women Wait for Liberty?*—and say nothing.

ROUND THREE

HOW LONG MUST WOMEN WAIT FOR LIBERTY?

Day after day, groups of women take turns as "Silent Sentinels." They stand eight hours a day, six days a week. It's a first! *Picketing the president? That's not in the rules!*

It rains. They stand. It sleets. They stand. It snows. They stand.

Woodrow invites the ladies in for hot coffee.

They ignore him.

VOTES

MR. PRESIDENT YOU SAY "LIBERTY IS THE FUNDAMENTAL DEMAND OF THE HUMAN SPIRIT"

VOTES FOR WOMEN

The Daily News

WAR !

Newspapers across the country cover the pickets. Woodrow grows angry. One early spring day, over one thousand suffragists march around the White House.

That same spring, the United States enters World War I in Europe. Woodrow meets with foreign leaders, gives orders to generals, and rallies the country with speeches. He's too busy; he forgets to keep an eye on Alice, but he better watch out!

Sure enough, Alice sees her opening. She pummels Woodrow with his own words! Her Silent Sentinels carry banners quoting the president's wartime speeches on freedom.

The banners ask, *How can the president fight for democracy around the world when half his own citizens can't vote?*

It's a good question, folks. It looks like the president might be in trouble.

DING! END OF ROUND THREE.

IN WOODROW'S CORNER

Soldiers and sailors tear suffrage banners to tatters. Small boys throw eggs and rotten tomatoes, grown men push and choke the women. *How dare they bother the president in wartime?* The Silent Sentinels never fight back with their fists—they let themselves be dragged off. But they always return.

But Woodrow gets tough! Police arrest the suffragists for . . . for . . . for blocking the sidewalk!

Alice gets the longest sentence—seven months in a filthy, infested jail. She won't back down!

Guards keep her alone, away from all other prisoners. She stays on her feet!

ROUND FOUR

VOTES FOR WOMEN

DEMOCRACY REQUIRES VOTES

They shine bright lights in her eyes, won't let her sleep, and say she is crazy. No matter what they do, she will not quit!

Alice spins and catches Woodrow off guard. She stops eating.

More than one hundred fifty suffragists go to prison. Some are choked and beaten by guards. Others join Alice's hunger strike. Will these women *die* for the right to vote? People across the country want the president to *do* something.

IN ALICE'S CORNER

The suffragist cause gets stronger. More and more citizens disagree with Woodrow. Women all over the country help the war effort, Mr. President. So, why can't they vote?

The unbelievable happens, folks! Woodrow weakens.
He stumbles. He staggers. *DING!*
Do we have a new champion?

YES!

After more than four years in the ring with Alice Paul, Woodrow Wilson throws in the towel. On January 9, 1918, the president supports the suffrage amendment.

Now Alice and Woodrow fight on the same side. Congress passes the suffrage amendment, but at least thirty-six states need to approve it. Alice gives speeches. Woodrow writes letters. Together, they defend democracy and champion freedom.

And they don't quit until the
Nineteenth Amendment, granting
women the right to vote, finally
becomes law on August 26, 1920.

And the country changes forever.
Because of Alice,
because of Woodrow,
and their Fight of the Century!

NINETEENTH AMENDMENT,
ratified August 18, 1920

"The right of citizens of the United States to vote shall not be denied or abridged by the United States or by any State on account of sex."

AUTHOR'S NOTE

This year (2020) is the one hundredth anniversary of the ratification of the Nineteenth Amendment. It was a key victory in the ongoing fight for equality for America's women and girls. Elizabeth Cady Stanton and Susan B. Anthony first proposed a women's suffrage amendment to the Constitution in 1869. It was ignored for decades until Alice Paul and her group of suffragists decided to pressure Woodrow Wilson for his support, starting the day *before* he became president. Today, it's common to see pickets at the White House or at presidential events, but Alice and her suffragists were the first group to target a president to support their cause.

Alice's Quaker religion promoted freedom for men and women, blacks and whites; it also objected to violence. Alice was not raised to fight physically, but to speak out for social justice in all its forms. She joined the militant British suffrage movement while attending graduate school in England. When she returned home to the United States, she worked for suffrage with the National American Woman Suffrage Association (NAWSA). Over time, Alice disagreed with that organization's moderate (and up to that point, unsuccessful) tactics under leaders Carrie Chapman Catt and Anna Howard Shaw. Alice Paul wanted more outspoken, active protests and eventually separated from NAWSA in 1914.

With her good friend and colleague Lucy Burns, Alice founded and ran her own group which became The National Woman's Party (NWP). In planning the 1913 suffrage parade, Alice's belief in equality was tested. Leading African American suffragists like Mary Church Terrell and Ida B. Wells-Barnett encouraged black women's suffrage clubs and universities to participate in the parade. Alice originally supported their full participation. When many white women refused to march with black women, Alice's committee segregated African American suffragists at the back of the parade. Wells-Barnett ignored the order and marched with the white Chicago delegation. Women from a few states, Michigan, New York, and Delaware, marched as integrated groups. Alice's support of her organization's discriminatory actions damaged her historical reputation as a fighter for equal rights.

In the years following the parade, Alice was jailed, beaten, and force-fed for her beliefs—but she accomplished her original goal: a suffrage amendment to the US Constitution.

Why did women want the vote? Here are the first three of the sixteen reasons listed in the 1913 Suffrage Parade program: *1. Because it is right and fair that those who must obey the laws should have a voice in making them.*

2. *Because it is just that those who must pay taxes should have a vote as to the size of the tax and the way it should be spent.*
3. *Because the moral, educational, and humane legislation desired by women would be secured more easily if women had votes.*
Votes were the only way women could change their lives, their family's lives, and their country.

At first, women voted in much lower proportions than men, but women's suffrage did change the United States forever. In a 1999 poll of the American public, the Nineteenth Amendment came in second only to World War II as "the most important event of the [twentieth] century." Once women voted, elected officials listened. Women earned respect, education, and job opportunities. Today among registered voters, women outnumber men by the millions and have voted in higher proportions in every presidential election since 1980.

After fighting for so long against suffrage, Woodrow Wilson changed too. He said, "I deem it one of the greatest honors of my life that this great event, so stoutly fought for, for so many years, should have occurred during the period of my administration." At their first meeting, Woodrow told Alice that suffrage had "never been brought to his attention." That wasn't true. His three daughters—Margaret, Jessie, and Eleanor—supported women's suffrage. Jessie was especially active in the movement, joining suffrage organizations, attending meetings, writing letters, and working for ratification.

Much later, Alice called Woodrow "a very great man." She continued to work for women's rights her whole life. She became a lawyer and in 1923 authored the Equal Rights Amendment (ERA). It states, "Equality of rights under the law shall not be denied or abridged by the United States or by any State on account of sex." It guarantees constitutional equality for both women and men throughout the United States. For the next fifty years, Alice and other activists fought for passage of the ERA. In 1972, it passed Congress, but was ratified by only thirty-five of the needed thirty-eight states. When it did not become law, five states voted to rescind their ratification. The ERA is again in the news—Nevada ratified it in 2017, then Illinois in 2018. You can find a complete list of current state ratification at equalrightsamendment.org. There is still much work to be done until we have freedom and equality for all.

A BRIEF TIMELINE OF WOMEN'S SUFFRAGE IN THE UNITED STATES

1776 — Declaration of Independence (July) founds the United States of America.

1787 — Constitutional Convention gives each state power over voting rights. Women who could previously vote lose that right in all states except New Jersey.

1791 — The Bill of Rights is adopted, but voting is not addressed. (In most states, women, African Americans, and Native Americans can't vote. Many states also require property ownership, literacy, or religious affiliations.)

1807 — New Jersey revokes women's right to vote.

1848 — First Woman's Rights Convention, Seneca Falls, NY, "to discuss the social, civil, and religious condition of woman." (Women's rights leaders begin to organize on a national level.)

1861–1865 — The Civil War. Women's rights groups prioritize war efforts and abolition of slavery over suffrage. Thirteenth Amendment abolishes slavery in 1865.

1867 — Woman suffrage defeated in Kansas and New York.

1868 — Fourteenth Amendment ratified. It ensures legal protections, includes African Americans, excludes Native Americans (who do not become citizens or vote until 1924). Defines citizens as males.

1869 — Elizabeth Cady Stanton and Susan B. Anthony found the National Woman Suffrage Association (NWSA). NWSA opposes the proposed Fifteenth Amendment because it doesn't include women. Lucy Stone founds the American Woman Suffrage Association (AWSA), which supports the Fifteenth Amendment. Wyoming Territory grants women suffrage.

1870 — Fifteenth Amendment ratified. It guarantees voting rights to all male citizens including African Americans. Utah Territory grants women suffrage.

1871 — The Anti-Suffrage Society is formed.

1874 — Woman suffrage defeated in Michigan.

1877 — Woman suffrage defeated in Colorado.

1882 — Woman suffrage defeated in Nebraska.

1883 — Washington Territory grants women suffrage.

1884 — Woman suffrage defeated in Oregon.

1887 — Montana Territory grants women suffrage. Woman suffrage defeated in Rhode Island.

1889 — Woman suffrage defeated in Washington State.

1890 — NWSA and AWSA merge to become NAWSA (National American Woman Suffrage Association), which increases efforts supporting state suffrage laws with limited success. Wyoming becomes the first state to grant women suffrage. Woman suffrage defeated in South Dakota.

1893 — Colorado grants women suffrage.

1896 — Utah and Idaho grant women suffrage. Woman suffrage defeated in California.

1902 — Woman suffrage defeated in New Hampshire.

1910 — Alice Paul returns to the US to continue suffrage work begun in England (January) and speaks at NAWSA's annual convention (April). Washington State grants women suffrage. Woman suffrage defeated in Oklahoma.

1911 — California grants women suffrage.

1912 — Arizona, Oregon, and Kansas grant women suffrage. Woman suffrage defeated in Ohio and Wisconsin.

1913 — Woman Suffrage Procession, Washington, DC (March 3). Woodrow Wilson inaugurated twenty-eighth president (March 4). First delegations of suffragists meet with Wilson (March 17). Alice Paul with Lucy Burns founds the Congressional Union (CU) for Woman Suffrage, part of NAWSA (April). Alaska Territory grants women suffrage. Illinois grants partial suffrage.

Woman suffrage procession, Washington, DC, March 3, 1913

1914 — Alice Paul's CU separates from NAWSA over her organization's forceful tactics. Montana and Nevada grant women suffrage. Woman suffrage defeated in Missouri and North Dakota.

1915 — Woman suffrage defeated in Massachusetts, New Jersey, and Pennsylvania.

1916 — CU forms the Woman's Party (WP), composed of women who have voting rights, to help secure the suffrage amendment. CU and WP merge into one organization, the National Woman's Party (NWP), in June. Woodrow Wilson reelected (November). Woman suffrage defeated in Iowa and West Virginia.

1917 — Silent picketing of the White House begins (January). Grand Picket around White House before Wilson's second inauguration (March). US enters World War I (April). Arrests, fines, and imprisonment of picketers begin (June). Alice Paul hunger strikes and is force-fed, other suffragists beaten and tortured at Occoquan Workhouse in Virginia (November). New York grants women suffrage. Nebraska, Ohio, Indiana, North Dakota, and Rhode Island grant partial suffrage. Woman suffrage defeated in Maine.

Silent Sentinels picket line, February 1917

1918 — Suffrage amendment passes the House (January 10) but loses in the Senate by two votes. Wilson publicly declares support for the suffrage amendment (January 19). Jailed suffragists released, and arrests declared illegal (March). Wilson addresses the Senate supporting the suffrage amendment (September). World War I ends (November). Michigan, South Dakota, and Oklahoma grant women suffrage. Iowa, Maine, Minnesota, Missouri, Tennessee, and Wisconsin grant partial suffrage. Woman suffrage defeated in Louisiana.

1919 — NWP watchfire demonstrations begin, suffragists burn Wilson's speeches in an urn outside the White House. Suffrage amendment passes the Senate, and White House picketing ends (June). Struggle for ratification by at least two-thirds of the states (thirty-six of forty-eight) begins. Wisconsin becomes first state to ratify the Nineteenth Amendment (June).

1920 — Tennessee becomes the thirty-sixth state to ratify the amendment (August 18). The Nineteenth Amendment (Susan B. Anthony Amendment) becomes law (August 26).

BIBLIOGRAPHY*

"5,000 Women March, Beset by Crowds." *New York Times*, March 4, 1913. query.nytimes.com/mem/archive-free/pdf?res=9800E4DF1F3AE633A25757C0A9659C946296D6CF.

Adams, Katherine H., and Michael L. Keene. *Alice Paul and the American Suffrage Campaign.* Urbana: University of Illinois Press, 2008.

Baker, Jean H. "Endgame." Chap. 5 in *Sisters: The Lives of America's Suffragists.* New York: Hill & Wang, 2005.

Barber, Lucy. "A 'National' Demonstration: The Woman Suffrage Procession and Pageant, March 3, 1913." Chap. 2 in *Marching on Washington: The Forging of an American Political Transition.* Berkeley: University of California Press, 2002.

Behn, Beth. "Woodrow Wilson's Conversion Experience: The President and the Federal Woman Suffrage Amendment." Dissertation, University of Massachusetts, Amherst, 2012. scholarworks.umass.edu/cgi/viewcontent.cgi?article=1503&context=open_access_dissertations.

Bland, Sidney. "New Life in an Old Movement: Alice Paul and the Great Suffrage Parade of 1913 in Washington, D.C." Records of the Columbia Historical Society, Washington, DC, 71/72: 657–78.

Brown, Victoria Bissell. "Did Woodrow Wilson's Gender Politics Matter?" In *Reconsidering Woodrow Wilson: Progressivism, Internationalism, War, and Peace,* edited by John Milton Cooper Jr., 125-162, Washington, DC: Woodrow Wilson Center Press, 2008.

Byker, Carl, and Mitch Wilson, dir. *Woodrow Wilson.* An American Experience. Alexandria, VA: DVD. PBS Home Video, 2002.

"Colby Proclaims Woman Suffrage." *New York Times*, August 27, 1920, p. 1. nytimes.com/learning/general/onthisday/big/0826.html?mcubz=0.

Congressional Record. 62nd Cong. 3,922 (1912). Washington, DC: US Government Printing Office.

Cooney, Robert. *Winning the Vote: The Triumph of the American Woman Suffrage Movement.* Santa Cruz, CA: American Graphic Press, 2005.

Crenshaw, Abby. "A Political Union: The Relationship of Alice Paul and Woodrow Wilson." Nashville: *Journal of Student Historical Research.* tnstate.edu/history/journal/Abby%20Crenshaw.pdf.

"Fact Sheet: Gender Differences in Voter Turnout." Center for American Women and Politics, Rutgers, the State University of New Jersey, 2015. cawp.rutgers.edu/sites/default/files/resources/genderdiff.pdf.

Flexner, Eleanor, and Ellen Fitzpatrick. *Century of Struggle: The Woman's Rights Movement in the United States.* Cambridge, MA: Belknap Press, 1996.

Frost-Knappman, Elizabeth, and Kathryn Cullen-DuPont. *Women's Suffrage in America.* Eyewitness History. New York: Facts on File, 2005, pp. 301–5 and 329–33.

Gallagher, Robert S. "I Was Arrested, Of Course . . ." *American Heritage* 25, no. 2, (February 1974): pp. 16–24. americanheritage.com/content/%E2%80%9Ci-was-arrested-course%E2%80%A6%E2%80%9D.

Graham, Sara Hunter. "Woodrow Wilson, Alice Paul, and the Woman Suffrage Movement." *Political Science-Quarterly* 98, no. 4 (Winter 1983–84): 665–768.

Harvey, Sheridan. "Marching for the Vote: Remembering the Woman Suffrage Parade of 1913." Library of Congress, American Memory. memory.loc.gov/ammem/awhhtml/aw01e/aw01e.html.

Irwin, Inez Haynes. *The Story of Alice Paul and the National Women's Party.* Fairfax, VA: Denlinger's Publishers, 1964.

Lunardini, Christine A., and Thomas J. Knock. "Woodrow Wilson and Women's Suffrage: A New Look." *Political Science-Quarterly* 95, no. 4 (1980-81): 655–71.

Moore, Sarah J. "Making a Spectacle of Suffrage: The National Woman Suffrage Pageant, 1913." *Journal of American Culture* 20, no. 1 (1997): 89–103.

* *Websites active at time of publication*

National American Woman Suffrage Association. *Official Program Woman Suffrage Procession*. Washington, DC, (March 3, 1913).

Newport, Frank, David W. Moore, and Lydia Saad. "The Most Important Events of the Century from the Viewpoint of the People." Gallup News Service, December 6, 1999. gallup.com/poll/3427/most-important-events-century-from-viewpoint-people.aspx.

"Parade Struggles to Victory Despite Disgraceful Scenes." *Woman's Journal and Suffrage News* 44, no. 10 (March 8, 1913), p. 1.

Paul, Alice. "Conversations with Alice Paul: Woman Suffrage and the Equal Rights Amendment." By Amelia Fry. Suffragists Oral History Project, University of California, Berkeley, 1976. content.cdlib.org/view?docId=kt6f59n89c&doc.view=entire_text.

"President Talks to Deputation." *Woman's Journal and Suffrage News* 44, no. 12 (March 22, 1913).

"Report of the Woman's Rights Convention," Seneca Falls, July 19 and 20, 1848. nps.gov/wori/learn/historyculture/report-of-thewomans-rights-convention.

Stiehm, Jamie. "Woodrow Wilson Versus the Suffragettes." *U.S. News & World Report*, Dec. 10, 2013. usnews.com/opinion/blogs/Jamie-Stiehm/2013/12/10/woodrow-wilson-versus-the-suffrage-movement.

Stovall, James Glen. *Seeing Suffrage: The 1913 Washington Suffrage Parade, Its Pictures, and Its Effects on the American Political Landscape*. Knoxville: University of Tennessee Press, 2013.

"Suffragists See Wilson." *New York Times*, March 18, 1913, p. 2.

"Suffragists Will Picket White House." *New York Times*, January 10, 1917, p. 1.

von Garnier, Katja, dir. *Iron Jawed Angels*. New York. DVD. HBO Films, 2004.

Walton, Mary. *A Woman's Crusade: Alice Paul and the Battle for the Ballot*. Basingstoke, UK: Palgrave MacMillan, 2010.

wilsoncenter.org

Women of Protest: Photographs from the Records of the National Woman's Party. Library of Congress, American Memory. loc.gov/collections/static/women-of-protest/images/detchron.pdf.

"Women's Party to Call a Convention," *New York Times*, September 11, 1920, p. 2.

"Wonders Worked in Washington." *Woman's Journal and Suffrage News* 44, no. 9 (March 1, 1913).

Zahniser, J.D., and Amelia R. Fry. *Alice Paul: Claiming Power*. Cambridge: Oxford University Press, 2014.

SOURCE NOTES

"Unless women are prepared . . .": Paul, quoted in "Women's Party to Call a Convention," *New York Times*, September 11, 1920, p. 2.

"The man who is swimming . . .": Wilson, quoted in *Congressional Record*.

"The right of citizens of . . .": Nineteenth Amendment to the Constitution.

"The most important . . .": Newport, Moore, and Saad.

"Because it is right . . .": National American Woman Suffrage Association.

"I deem it one of . . .": Wilson, quoted in "Colby Proclaims Woman Suffrage."

"never been brought . . .": Wilson, quoted in Irwin, p. 34.

"a very great man": Paul/Fry, p. 92.

"To discuss the . . .": "Report of the Woman's Rights Convention."

"To me there is . . .": Paul, quoted in Gallagher, p. 24.

For those who still fight for women's rights.
"To me there is nothing complicated about
ordinary equality." —Alice Paul
—BR

For my parents, who have always fought for me
and worked to give the next generation a better future.
—SG

ACKNOWLEDGMENTS

Thanks to Lucienne Beard, executive director of the Alice Paul Institute, and historian Kris Myers for their perceptive comments on both text and art. Additional thanks to Celia Caust-Ellenbogen of the Swarthmore College Archives and Sarah Elichko, social sciences & data librarian at the Swarthmore College Library.

ABOUT THE ART

The work and colors for this book were inspired by lithographs from the 1900s–1920s and old boxing advertisements and illustrations. The sharp, black lines were incorporated to give the story a sense of motion and activity, as well as to incorporate aesthetic themes from competition, given the book's title which also refers to many famous boxing matches of the twentieth and twenty-first centuries.

PICTURE CREDITS

Library of Congress, Prints and Photographs Division: LC-DIG-hec-06897: 34; LC-USZ62-13028: 35; LC-USZ62-22262: 37 (top); LC-USZ62-31799: 37 (bottom).

Calkins Creek
An Imprint of Boyds Mills & Kane
calkinscreekbooks.com
Printed in China

ISBN: 978-1-62979-908-7
Library of Congress Control Number: 2019939632

First edition

10 9 8 7 6 5 4 3 2 1

Design by Barbara Grzeslo
The text is set in Futura.
The illustrations are done digitally.